My Darling Derry

Letter-poems about Derek Richter

founder of

The Mental Health Foundation

by

Sally Festing

Fair Acre Press

First published in Great Britain in 2019 by Fair Acre Press

www.fairacrepress.co.uk

A CIP catalogue record for this book is available from the British Library

ISBN 978-1-911048-35-0

Printed and bound by Lightning Source

Lightning Source has received Chain of Custody (CoC) certification from:
The Forest Stewardship CouncilTM (FSC®)
Programme for the Endorsement of Forest CertificationTM (PEFCTM) The Sustainable Forestry Initiative® (SFI®).

Front Cover Image: from Left to Right - Ben and Eone with Derry

Back Cover Image: Derry with Sally

Typeset and Cover Design by Nadia Kingsley

Acknowledgements

With thanks to the editors of the following magazines and e-magazines in which some of the following poems have appeared: Agenda, Ink Sweat & Tears, Stand, Tears in the Fence.

And my special thanks to Moniza Alvi, Heidi Williamson, Peter Wallis, Stephen Eisenman, Julia Webb and her Norwich Stanza for all the help they've given me.

Sally Festing, January 2019

Preface

In response to mental health issues experienced by his two siblings, my father Derek Richter became a noted neuro-psychiatrist and founder of the Mental Health Research Fund (now Foundation).

For more than sixty years, the Foundation has funded pioneering research and challenged the status of mental health in the UK.

After his death, I inherited hundreds of family letters, diaries and medical notes that are the source of my poems.

They reveal how his personal life affected his dedication to discover the cause and treatment of mental illness, and how this became the driving force of his life.

Family Tree

The Richter Family

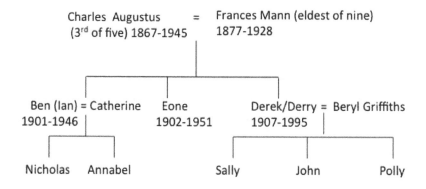

Charles Augustus (3rd of five) 1867-1945 = Frances Mann (eldest of nine) 1877-1928

Ben (Ian) = Catherine 1901-1946 — Eone 1902-1951 — Derek/Derry = Beryl Griffiths 1907-1995

Nicholas — Annabel

Sally — John — Polly

Contents

Their Prints

Moths, ghosts, my house is full of them.
I live with waves of silence but their lives
roar enormous through my rooms –
hung on walls, stuffed in bookcases, leaking
from wounded suitcases tied with string.

It rained last night, and the dead came down
with the drops – to gather where the land is flat
and windblown. The quiet stores their smiles.
I press my finger where theirs have been, thread
words to tumble them back, all talking, arguing.

Jottings
for Charles Richter

My father's father, clipped moustache, fair furrowed hair,
sighs into his notebook. His sighs fall
between lists, budgets, plans, addresses, sketches,
fragments of Nietzsche, rough drafts of plays,
Byron's lines and furniture designs.

The landscape skips and dives like an eyelid's flicker.
Always short of time, he shakes himself
free of the shrill note, tries to let the moment
open itself, but his mind keeps leaping
as his pencil riffs. *Get to the quick*, says his train.

Gold medals roll in. Rest is a forgotten flower.
He's concentrating as his train draws in.
His sighs drift between his glass coach and self-reproach.
I watch his pencil move. His elegant script breaks
into runs – minor expenses, regrets, yearnings.

'A state in which one sees things most decidedly as they are not' *Neitzsche*

Charles met Frances at Aberdeen's Grand Hotel.
Fired by Burns, her wits felt sharp as his own.
She was a beauty too. Her gaiety amazed.
But her freshness was thoroughbred. What did he expect.

It's tragic to see the longing slipped in
his sonnets, the letters, paintings, gifts.
Charles wasn't a partyman. For someone raised
to scrimp, she was extravagant.

And his mother's voice called back. She bid
her son to follow her among flower beds
where the brightest air brimmed.
What did he expect, out on his own?

Cabinet-Maker

Charles wants walnut burl, ebony for contrast;
establishing this, he turns to a new sheet
of his pocket sketchbook. His pencil moves fast.
Does his breath catch? Heartwood – a treat
of knots, mottled, rippled, and stained
to gold embroidery.

His table with two thick slab-legs braves the 'Twenties',
shaved and planed, everything stamped
with precision and progress. Already he dares
to dream how this beautiful thing will amplify
his dining room. Its black echoed in the carpet
he'll design, and in his twin sideboard. The spirit

of Bath will be reborn. He wants
to discover what he doesn't know,
wants his inwardness to flow clear
from the hand. Straight lines keep the heart
in check. Curved lines shape his art.
What really counts is the grain.

An Epistolary Challenge: from my Uncle Ben (aged 12) to his father, Charles, at Glasgow Central Station Hotel

May 1913   Cresthill, Lansdown Park, Bath

Dear Father

Just had some Glasgow Sugar Butter Melon Bake
Is there any more of it?
Not the cake, I mean the name.

Your letter had two mistakes.
One is mother's address in Somerset
The other (don't forget), I'll tell you

next time I write, unless you solve
the riddle: Gran and I found the Devil.
She said, *Don't catch its tail.*

Please can you send the house key?
I may need my white flannels on Wednesday
for the gym display.

I went to the Works but too late, you'd gone.
Do try and turn up on Saturday to the bazaar.
Yr loving son.

ps. The Devil is a stove
Gran found to burn rubbish.
pps. I'm Ben.

Spontaneous Notes from Frances to her husband, May 1913

Grosvenor Guesthouse, Clevedon

Darling Charles

The journey was all mist & appleblossom. I thought the line prettier
than last time, then understood. I was on the wrong train,
must go right back to Bristol.

Arrived at 9.45! tired, v cold & hungry because I'd had no lunch.
I wished you had been with me, not for the cold and hunger
but for the lights in darkness thick as silt.

I bargained with a cabby, five shillings to drive me here,
and he walked the last bit leading the horse. It was very slow.
Dearest, I must sleep now before I drop.

Afternoon: Dr C says I have bad Rheumatism. I'm very run down,
anaemic & generally out of sorts. His tonic will make me
sleep & stop neuralgic pain.

I'm glad to have your card. It's been heavenly here –
the tide out, all pale oyster colours,
the water still & brown & shimmering.

The house is quite comfy, they only charge me 25/-.
You could sketch on a Sunday,
the sea air would do you good.

Don't forget the children's Bazaar next weekend.
I miss you very much, likewise my darling chicks.
Kisses when I see you, lovingly F

Derek's Play

Like an echo, he's at home
long after the others. The last
child alone with his mother.

Charcoal, potassium nitrate, sulphur.

D. Richter: Firework Display
January 4, after tea on Saturday
ALL MY OWN FIREWORKS.

A Message from Frances to her Daughter Eone, 1916

My darling little girl,
Are you better, and getting to lessons?
I hoped to come and see you but have been very unwell.

Derry & I gathered a huge bunch of orchids & cowslips
                                        from the field.
We spotted a weasel by the hedge, & the nesting birds
in the front garden can nearly fly.

All our hens have chicks. Two under the fowl house,
three darkish ones in the old cock's home,
& four nearby – white as cottonwool.

I cradled them in a basket & tried to feed the babies
but they wouldn't eat, so tonight I shall tuck them
under their mummy.

Daddy is in London. Mrs C has done the rooms.
Derry & I are alone in this huge house,
I must manage the ironing somehow.

Much love to you dear child. I think of you very often
& want my little girl to grow strong & well.
Your loving Mother.

From Frances to her Husband at Manchester's Midland Hotel

3 April, 1916   Roseneath, Willsden, Bristol
My darling man,

I couldn't sleep without sending a little line –
I have been very unwell, hardly out of the house.
Yesterday was interminable, today your note.
You are a real Wagnerian, I have but to wish & lo!

That grim journey, you *must* travel first class
while the war is on, while you do good business.
Eggs are dear everywhere, somehow I must try
to borrow £1, the villain wanted 2/6 for hot cross-buns.

Ben writes "Shall I have pocket money Easter week?"
How I wish I could hug the boy, I miss him so.
Eone wants you to come back soon.
Derry is happy as a bird and *very* busy.

I think sometimes I would heal if I could just get out,
if I could forget the effort of each day. Imagine
coming back to everything fresh, the effect
it would have on my heart to be sprung

once again by the joy of each season. To pick up
the little bone-white driftwood bits of my life
and be restored.
                              Yours lovingly, F

The Hang of Things: from Ben to his Home

St Edwards, Oxford   9 October, 1916
Dear All,

Thank you for the ripping box of tuck,
also the iron pills.

I draw chiefly flowers, in pencil and charcoal.
The master says they're well done.

But no, Father, I haven't carpentered –
Mother forgot to sign the extras list.

Greek is better in the upper division.
I'm 1st in our form for maths.

Over 100 of us went to pack Government stores
from huge iron sheds outside Didcot.

Just think, 80,000 stretchers alone!
Think where they're bound, the stink, the hurt.

We left by train, with slabs of bread 'n' cheese.
Slaved 1.30 till 5.00. Cleared 20 trucks.

Is there news about our company shares?
If not I must try my money in Exchequer Bonds.

Time to sharpen pruning knives so I can do the trees.
With best love, Ben.

Derek's Diary

'PRIVATE'
you scored the cover
in the protective upper case.

Page after page, in pencil or pen.

Withholding cash when you were anxious
was as ingrained as the call to record your moods.

*   *   *

In the pump room, hooked
on Dvorak's 'Song to the Moon'.

And out into the garden.

All year you tinkered with electric motors.

I start this diary in 1921 at the age of 14. Tidied up my den. Allotted a box in which to keep my valuables such as War Saving Certificates. Awful slump in the trade, must economise in everything.

To Bonnets with E.
Tea with a scone cost 2 shillings, but for us the girl took 5 pence off.

I will cost him a lot at Oundle.

* * *

Piano practice 45 mins every day.

Helped Pater plant bluebells.
Picked flowers for Mother.

Lead burning on my accumulator plate.
Used iodine. "Everyday Science" arrived.

In summer, you half-liked your loneliness.

*   *   *

Nothing was ever simple with you
so you didn't know how partisan you'd become.

Your sister had begun to doubt her sanity,
so you had to hold on to your own.

Ben went back to Oxford.
Cut wood for the studio fire but could not make it light.

Fitting for new uniform.

Continued to tidy my den.
I'm in rather a funk about meeting the boys.

*   *   *

Of course Dad didn't hit her back.
I know she isn't well but she eats chicken while we eat cheese.
He is boss of 4 firms, yet she will ruin him —

In Oxford, I wore trousers for the first time,
Ben said "you don't half look a blood".

Woken at 4.am by Eone whispering "prowlers".
Put on coat, took my life-preserver, loaded dad's rifle but we didn't find
anyone. Slept till 10 o'clock when the bobby called.

Derek's List

'Things to do'

Carpentering. Carving.
Drawing. Gardening.
Pumping. Painting,
Plasterceen. Charcoaling.
Go bicycling. Go fishing
(catch the Roach).
Meccano. Reading.
Make water wheel.
Make Electricity.
A steam engine.
A rabbit cage. A pond.
Make for the POST-WAR-CONCERT.
Design Bird traps.
Fretwork. Make a gun.

Eone to her Mother: The Thin Line

Bathwick Hill House, Bath   11 October, 1921

My Dearest Mother,
I expect you think me a very undutiful daughter.
I have often tried to write, only to be interrupted.
I think Poppa has mentioned that I've been unwell.

I have been disgusted with the world in general
and the servants trouble me. Sometimes I thought
I was going mad! It may be foolish but I dwell on it

until the line between insanity and saneness
seems frightfully thin. My nightmare is over for now
and today Heaven's gates seem opened wide.

Wasn't it topping of Poppa to take us to the Bristol concert?
Godfrey, this awfully decent young chap,
told the Operatic Society I'm "exceedingly musical!"

I have so often wished you were home from Weisbaden
to share our happiness and sadness.
Hope you will be *much* better by the time
this reaches you. Ever yr. loving Eone

Eone Confides in her Younger Brother, Derek

At the Academy I try to paint
the rhyming shapes and patterns of the sky.
Father comes home and wants to help. But why
does he criticise? It isn't meant

to hurt. Derry, what can I do?
The birds make scales and set off an alarm,
it splits my head. I burn
and belt it in. Then come to you.

My fingers fumble the piano, it's a strain.
The servants leave early when Mother's away.
Father makes his worries mine. I hear him say
'Oh dear, milk pudding again'.

I mustn't worry Mother.
Sometimes death seems the only way
to solve the problem – how to fly.
Will she hear my voice shut altogether?

Last night Father grabbed my hand, roused
for what he called a moonlight spin.
I can't go on, I'm angry but can't tell him.
This is crazyland. A madhouse.

Full Steam: from Charles to his Son Ben, 1921

Dear old Fellow
Three nights without stripping underwear, or bed. I almost live
on the railways, and they are living on me! Grace to the triumph
of modern locomotion, we'll reach Manchester in an hour,
then on to Bradford, Leeds, Edinburgh, Glasgow. After Mother,
Derry & Uncle B, write I unto you from a jerky train.

On Sunday, I splashed watercolour about with Eone.
I try to give her my best advice though it sometimes seems she hangs
the sun at the angle she needs it. At Keynsham she rehearsed
Ruddigore – she's not robust and I don't know what to suggest
about singing lessons. I'm doing pastels too but need paler shades.

Mother writes that her own health improves, only 'it will take
a long time etc. etc.' I profoundly hope this is true and that she will not
lapse into her former state. Her doctor cautions her not to travel home
until the spring. She says her recovery depends on me.
I think it depends most of all upon her.

Yesterday, in a crowded committee room, the discourse
was as fiery as the temperature. I gave them the gee-up
and was called 'mercenary' for trying to talk business
rather than make pretty speeches. People get prickly
when asked for money.

I ponder 'Einstein', some of which embodies truths I found
in 1890. As to Time being a new dimension, what say you?
I envy you at Die Meistersingers, truly one of Wagner's
most tuneful operas. Local experts were unanimous
at the gramophone show - the Megaphone hails the future.

Just now, it's Hardy makes me long for the blackbird.
To be alone with its song. Is it happy & workish
with you at Oxford? Don't get run down. I dealt with my cold
and exorcised my demon, indigestion. Can now eat everything

and I often feel like it! This monster munches through red trees
and a withering Autumn sky. Much love, Father

Charles Wrestles with his Inability to Control

My dear Ben,   14 June 1923

Mother's letters, like your own
are very few, and no word
from that sister of yours for a fortnight.

I left Eone heading for Étaples,
a little wistful,
yet she found it "trés swish".

You know your sister, stirred giddy
by a tutor's compliments.
Now she wants to say bigger things.

Glad to hear from you, I was rather in the dumps.
Labour problems add to the usual claims of business.
Well Cheerio old fellow, Father

Market Scene

Eone maps in the orange sunshades
opening across her sketch
like harvest moons, raising such hopes in her –
little throbs inside her dream.
Étaples Market she'll call it
when she dares to colour in.

There's a vertical strip of sky between
blocks of building, vivid behind the throb
of bartering, banks of food for sale,
thrusting hawkers, aproned women
in small white caps and widow's weeds
(the endless grief of World War I) –
a picture fixed already in her head.

Above all, there's her tutor. His presence
brings the very soul of market closer,
for she's not met a man like him
to love. For a moment her yearning
comes on like madness.
It's like jumping off her moons

onto the sun. The next move matters,
let's say it's a high cliff leap.
She rests her pencil. Sighs. The sketch
is ready. She stands. Reaches to touch
the sky. This buoyant June
she could kiss a stranger.

Eone's Tutor

Your painting is better than mine, he said
and his words reached out and felt like love.
He believed in her strength – where it might lead
and his words made music, and music moves.

His words reached out and felt like love,
Come to Paris with me, he said.
His words made music, and music moves.
So they shared a bed.

Come to Paris with me, he said.
If a voice hadn't hissed 'adultery'
they'd have stayed together, shared a bed.
But afterwards, she could only cry.

If a voice hadn't whispered 'adultery',
she'd believe in her strength and where it led,
but after, she could only cry.
Your painting is better than mine, he said.

My Aunt Eone's Voices

'The insane startle us with their metaphors and with their occasional searing truths.' Dannie Abse

After Paris, her lover's wife smacked her
back into her own grass.

After that her father lectured
'honour'.

After a moment of lostness
she ran to a cliff by the sea.

After her fall,
voices clawed her mind.

*

They talked about a man who touched me.
The police must get this right.

They used a looking glass the other side of the sheet.
They said they were talking to my heart.

Where is Dr Craig? Why is he not here?
An electric force inside me gives me pain.

I believe my father is behind the scenes.
Why am I treated as if I am insane?

*

Afterwards, the Consultant signed
and took away her words.

Like an escalator, she folded into nothing.

Frances Writes to my Father, 1924

My darling Derry, it's all so sad. We brought Eone home
and I had to engage a nurse, but she's dreadfully unhappy.
So I cry & cry & wish ...
Grandmother, I read your words
with the clarity distance brings
and wish you'd had a simpler mission.

I should just love to see you at Oundle, dear.
I need a change badly and it would be better for Eone.
I am the only one who can manage her
& she needs some humouring I can tell you.
Night & day. I am so worn out I have little spirit left.
Frances, it's all so sad.

And how do your words –
the almost illegible pages, bear on
your youngest, schoolboy son?
It is terribly hard to see the poor child suffer
& she is vexed if I look ill or cry. I'd willingly
give my life to make her well, but if I can't...

Darling, the garden is simply heavenly.
At 5.30 I picked flowers for Eone's breakfast tray.
I have been very unwell but now feel more cheerful.
So glad of your letter. I hope you are not quite dropping
your piano playing. I too love Beethoven best.
Always he played the piano – the past came alive

in his hands. And reading Frances' letters
brings the past alive in mine.
All the earth is brown & the rain makes the colours bright –
an odd gleam of sun is like the smile on a bairn's face.
A week ago the leaves were every shade of sunset.
Now the trees are nearly bare, the leaves are falling falling.

In which Charles Speaks of his Sadness

Voices steal her mind,
wrestle with her brain.
Where will it end?

The Question of Uncle Ben's Balance

i.

I was stuck   on a tightrope
under   huge unleafy trees

Weeping for my sister   I looked down
but I wobbled   god I wobbled

We were all   shattered
by her shattering   No one guessed

the wretchedness   I buried in my head
the sting   of what

I wouldn't admit   my barefoot steps
along the lines   the damage they bring

ii.

Gentle, sweet, good-mannered Ben.
You read the Bible end to end.

For a brief equilibrium,
you moved to the big house.

How you loved the grapes that draped
the conservatory, the Beauties of Bath

you pruned. The garden of rocks
you hauled up stone by stone.

The carvings you chiselled
in hardest wood.

Catherine was a gift
and your heart drowned in her –

As hedge sparrows made love
you toed the tightrope.

iii.

War
      and the whole earth cracked.
I wanted a trigger.

I tipped. I lost my hair.
Trees were my hair whipped stiff.

Like a blind white larva that couldn't pupate,
I was breakable but I didn't give in.

No one knew how madly I gambled.
I tried to walk on my hands.

Articles went missing.
Was it me the gardener saw
wandering aimlessly in town?

iv.

Stuck in some accident of time,
you hallucinated.
Your face changed shape (the vertigo).
You wore a mask.
But your body's pain was paper-thin
and disposable.

A shudder under your pale
bleached skull.
A shift in the hollow of your head.
Your heart's
stone
weighed you down. The rope
stretched
and sagged, dropping you

Derek Makes a Commitment

They tried testosterone.
They tried electric shock.
The block in my brother's brain

was adamant. My sister too,
after thyroid, after prolan.
Sunk in the depths

of her silence.
First one, then two.
My sorrow.

Work. Work.
Funds to be raised,
we must nurse research,

shrink their shame.
Committed, I'll hunt down
the causes of their curse.

A Poetry of Release

with a debt to WS Graham

Derek's efforts ran unhindered as the rain.
Those dearest to him from childhood

gone, he thought grief a gift he should earn.
There's relatively little words can do for grief

but what else did he have?
There were, he knew, huge worlds to share. Explore.

*

Let this poem be a still thing, a mountain
constructed from glass. I begin with

the ghost of an intention which blasts itself
to nurture a new collision.

Perhaps the shape of us – the wreckage,
the shame and the dance – is in our language.

Notes

30   Eone's pastel hangs within sight of my writing table.

31   Eone's tutor was the accomplished artist, Leonard Richmond
      (1889-1965).

32   Eone's speech is extracted from five handwritten pages, a
      transcript of her words by her Consultant, Ernest White at
      Fairfield Nursing home, 9.1.1925. Three times, she mentions
      Dr Craig. I believe this was Sir Maurice Craig KBE FRCP (1866-
      1935), pioneer in mental illness and Virginia Woolf's psychiatrist.

34   Eone's psychosis developed in 1924 when she was 22, Ben was
      then 23, Derek, 17.

38   Most of Ben's adult woodcarvings were bought by the Cunard
      liners and his designs for interiors were illustrated in the Studio
      Yearbooks and elsewhere.

39   Ben was sectioned at the age of 45 and died two years later.

41   Derek wrote: 'Eone's sensitive schizoid personality was well
      defined … she should have been encouraged in healthy ways of
      living. Ben's illness appeared schizophrenic, though not typical …
      There was no evidence of significant abnormality until the war
      period, when he showed several forms of regression to childish
      habits of response… prefrontal leucotomy was also tried but
      tended to make him worse, and he degenerated into the most
      sorry condition.'